CATS

and other mammals

Sally Morgan

Belitha Press

First published in the UK in 2001 by

Belitha Press Limited, London House,
Great Eastern Wharf, Parkgate Road,
London SW11 4NQ

Copyright © Belitha Press Limited 2001
Text by Sally Morgan

Includes specialist photography by Robert Pickett

With thanks to Croydon Cats Protection

Editor: Russell McLean
Designer: Jacqueline Palmer
Educational consultant: Emma Harvey,
    Honeywell Infants School, London

ISBN 1 84138 311 2

Printed in Hong Kong

10 9 8 7 6 5 4 3 2 1

British Library Cataloguing in Publication Data
for this book is available from the British Library.

Picture acknowledgements:
Karl Ammann/Ecoscene: 17t. Animals Unlimited: 20b. A.N.T./NHPA: front cover
tr, 26c. Steve Austin/Papilio: 9b. Jim Bain/NHPA: 20t. E. J. Bent/Ecoscene: 25b.
Jane Burton: back cover, 1, 6t, 6b, 11t, 13bl, 14b, 15b, 16t, 18t. Gerald Lasz/Still
Pictures: 23b. John Liddiard/Ecoscene: 27c. Neeral Mishra/Ecoscene: 25t, 26t.
Sally Morgan/Ecoscene: 23t. Papilio: front cover c, 4t, 4b, 5c, 5b, 15t, 17b, 18b,
19c, 19b, 23c, 28b, 29cl. Ken Preston-Mafham/Premaphotos: 13br. Robin Redfern/
Ecoscene: 5t, 7b, 21cl. Louise Rodgers/Ecoscene: 27b. Kjell Sandved/Ecoscene:
11b, 26b. S. Tiwari/Ecoscene: 21r.

All other photography by Robert Pickett.

Every attempt has been made to clear copyrights but should there be
inadvertent omissions please apply to the publisher for rectification.

Contents

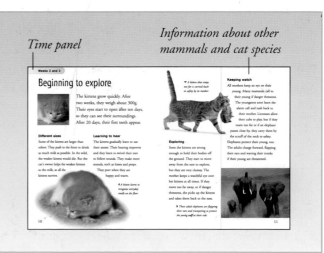

This book is about the life cycle of the domestic cat. Panels at the top of the pages show when each stage in the cat's life cycle takes place. The sections on a yellow background give information about the life cycles of other mammals as well as other cat species.

Words in **bold** are explained in the glossary on page 30.

What is a cat?

A cat is a **mammal**. Its body is covered in hair. Cats give birth to live young called kittens. The kittens feed on their mother's milk for the first weeks of their lives.

▲ *A cat can jump distances up to six times its own body length. It pushes off with its back legs and lands on its front paws.*

Meat-eaters

Domestic cats belong to a group of mammals called **carnivores**. These are mammals which eat meat. The group includes dogs, bears, raccoons, weasels and wild cats, too. Carnivores are **predators**, which means that they hunt and kill other animals for food.

◀ *A young cat plays with a toy. When it grows older, the cat will hunt small animals.*

Running and jumping

A cat has a slim but muscular body which is perfect for hunting. It has a bendy, or flexible, spine which allows it to run, jump and climb easily. A cat has excellent senses of sight and smell to find its **prey**.

From kitten to cat

A newborn kitten is small and helpless. Even at this early age, the kitten looks like a cat. During the first weeks of its life it is looked after by its mother, who feeds and cleans it. The kitten grows quickly and reaches adult size within six months. While the kitten is with its mother, it has to learn how to hunt and how to behave with other cats.

▲ *A wildcat looks like a large **tabby** cat.*

Wild relations

Domestic cats are related to wild cats such as lions, tigers, leopards, wildcats and bobcats. Some of the larger wild cats can run at great speeds to catch their prey, especially the cheetah, which is the fastest land animal. Lions hunt together in groups because they are heavier and cannot run so fast.

▶ *The bobcat is the most common wild cat in North America.*

5

A kitten is born

Cats give birth to live young, like most other mammals. In the days before the kittens are born, the mother cat finds a safe place to use as a nest.

▲ *A cat gives birth to her kittens one by one.*

▼ *The newborn kittens stay close to their mother for warmth.*

Large litters

There are usually five or six kittens in a **litter**. They are born one after another, about 20 minutes apart. As soon as each kitten is born, the mother cat licks it clean. A newborn kitten weighs about as much as an orange – between 100g and 150g. The kitten's eyes are shut and it is deaf. It is too weak to hold up its head and it can barely crawl. The kitten is very **sensitive** to temperature. The first thing it does is to crawl towards the warmth of its mother and the other kittens.

Drinking milk

When all of the kittens have been born, they take their first drink of milk. Their mother has ten **nipples** on the underside of her body.

She nudges the kittens towards her nipples. The kittens suck milk from them. She makes sure that each kitten finds a nipple and drinks her milk.

◀ *The cat stretches out so that all her kittens can **suckle**, or drink her milk.*

Building a nest

Many wild mammals look for a dry, warm place to give birth to their young. It has to be a safe place, hidden from predators. Small mammals, such as mice and voles, creep into holes where they build a nest from grass and other warm materials. Newborn mice are small, blind and hairless. They stay in the nest until their eyes open. The nest must keep them warm until they grow fur.

▲ *Newborn rats are blind and their pink bodies are hairless.*

The first week

Kittens are almost helpless for the first seven to ten days of their lives. They spend all day drinking and sleeping.

▲ *The kittens huddle together to stay warm.*

Smell and touch

The kittens huddle together, close to their mother. Their eyes are still shut, so they use their senses of smell and touch to find their way around. They crawl towards the smell of their mother's milk when they are hungry.

Then they use their sense of touch to find a nipple. They soon learn that more milk will flow if they press their mother's body around the nipple.

▼ *Each kitten takes a nipple in its mouth and sucks hard.*

Keeping clean

The mother cat keeps her kittens spotlessly clean. She spends much of the day licking them with her rough tongue. This helps to build a bond between mother and kitten. The kittens sleep close together, sometimes in a pile, to keep warm.

▲ *After the kittens have fed, the mother cleans each one with her rough tongue.*

At first, the only sounds the kittens can make are grunts and squeals. But, as their hearing improves, they make more sounds. Within a week, they make their first attempts to purr.

Up and running

The young of **grazing animals**, such as sheep, horses, antelope and zebra, can run around minutes after birth. As soon as they are born, the mother cleans them and nudges them to their feet for their first drink of milk. This is a very dangerous time for grazing animals that live on the African **savannah**, or grassland. During the birth, the mother is vulnerable to attack from lions and cheetahs. The youngsters cannot run very fast at first. Many of them are killed by big cats.

▼ *A young lamb suckles while its mother watches for predators such as foxes.*

Beginning to explore

The kittens grow quickly. After two weeks, they weigh about 300g. Their eyes start to open after ten days, so they can see their surroundings. After 20 days, their first teeth appear.

Different sizes

Some of the kittens are larger than others. They push to the front to drink as much milk as possible. In the wild, the weaker kittens would die. But the cat's owner helps the weaker kittens to the milk, so all the kittens survive.

Learning to hear

The kittens gradually learn to use their senses. Their hearing improves and they learn to swivel their ears to follow sounds. They make more sounds, such as hisses and peeps. They purr when they are happy and warm.

◀ *A kitten learns to recognize everyday smells on the floor.*

▼ A kitten that strays too far is carried back to safety by its mother.

Exploring

Soon the kittens are strong enough to hold their bodies off the ground. They start to move away from the nest to explore, but they are very clumsy. The mother keeps a watchful eye over her kittens at all times. If they move too far away, or if danger threatens, she picks up the kittens and takes them back to the nest.

Keeping watch

All mothers keep an eye on their young. Many mammals call to their young if danger threatens. The youngsters soon learn the alarm call and rush back to their mother. Lionesses allow their cubs to play, but if they roam too far or if an elephant passes close by, they carry them by the scruff of the neck to safety. Elephants protect their young, too. The adults charge forward, flapping their ears and waving their trunks if their **calves** are threatened (below).

Playtime

The kittens continue to grow.
Now they weigh about 500g.
They learn to use their tail for
balance and can walk easily. Soon
they are able to run in short bursts.

▲ *When a kitten has a few small
teeth, it is ready to eat solid food.*

A change of diet

For the first weeks of their lives, the
kittens' only food is their mother's
milk. They drink more and more
each day. The mother cat has to
eat much more food than normal.

This allows her to produce enough
milk for her fast-growing kittens.
After a month, the kittens have grown
several small teeth, so they can start to
eat solid food. This change in diet is
called **weaning**. At first, the kittens
just try out the solid food. Each day,
they eat more solid food and drink
less milk. But they will still take
some milk from their mother
for a few more weeks.

◀ *The kittens sniff
their food warily
before eating it.*

Rough and tumble

The kittens sleep for many hours each day, but they have short bursts of activity when they play with each other. Play is important in the life of a cat. This is when the kittens learn how to behave with each other and with their mother. If they play too roughly or hurt their mother, she cuffs them with her paw. Playing helps the kittens to improve their co-ordination skills, which makes them better hunters. They can chase a ball or string toy, but they can't quite follow it when it passes over their head.

The rough and tumble of play is important to both kittens (below) and lion cubs (right).

Learning from play

Lion and cheetah cubs play with their brothers and sisters. This is when they learn hunting tricks, such as how to creep up on their prey. They have fun, but it prepares them for living on their own, too. Play-fighting can look serious. Sometimes the cubs hurt each other, but they stop before any real damage is done.

Learning to hunt

Cats are born with the **instinct** to hunt. They have excellent senses and muscular bodies. Their claws and teeth are the perfect shape for hunting.

▲ *A kitten sharpens its claws on a special pole covered in rope.*

Curved claws

Cats have sharp, curved claws to catch and hold prey such as small birds, mice and voles. Unlike the claws of a dog, a cat's claws can be **retracted**.

This means they can be pulled back inside the toe. The claws have to be kept sharp. You might see a cat sharpening them on tree trunks or pieces of furniture.

◀ *Kittens love to pounce on moving objects.*

14

A cat has sharp teeth, too. The teeth at the front of its mouth are for biting off small pieces of food. They are called **incisors**. On either side of them is a large, sharp tooth called a **canine**. A cat uses its four canines to bite into prey, hold it and then rip it to pieces. Behind the canines are larger, flatter teeth called **premolars** and **molars**. These crush and break up food into smaller pieces that the cat can swallow.

▲ *This cat has killed a mouse by biting through the back of its neck.*

Killing prey

Cats catch small birds by creeping up on them. They move silently on their soft, padded paws. Sometimes they freeze to avoid being seen or heard. When they are near, they crouch down, waiting for the right moment to attack. Then they leap forwards and swat the bird to the ground.

▶ *Kittens learn to watch, pounce and catch when they play with their toys.*

Often, cats play with their prey until it lies still. Then they bite through the back of its neck to kill it. Cats are very patient – they may sit beside a hole for a long time, waiting for a mouse to appear.

Leaving home

By the time the kittens are about two months old they can feed and look after themselves. They have grown large enough to leave their mother and go to a new home.

▶ *A kitten that has just moved to a new home is very wary at first. It smells everything carefully.*

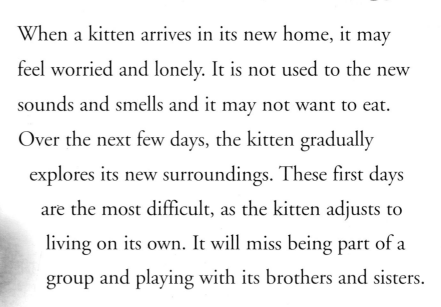

When a kitten arrives in its new home, it may feel worried and lonely. It is not used to the new sounds and smells and it may not want to eat. Over the next few days, the kitten gradually explores its new surroundings. These first days are the most difficult, as the kitten adjusts to living on its own. It will miss being part of a group and playing with its brothers and sisters.

◀ *This eight-week-old kitten is old enough to leave its mother.*

Staying or leaving

Female lion cubs, or lionesses, stay with their mother. They become permanent members of the **pride**, or family, and hunt with their mother and aunts. But their brothers have to leave. Each pride has only two or three male lions. The young males are chased away by the adult males.

The red fox leads a **solitary** life. A female fox has a litter of between three and six cubs. When the cubs are four weeks old, the mother takes them hunting. They are ready to leave their mother when they are eight weeks old. They have to move away and find somewhere else to live.

▶ *Foxes hunt at dusk and dawn. They eat small mammals such as mice and rabbits, as well as birds, worms and even berries.*

▲ *This elephant herd has several youngsters of different ages.*

Elephants live in herds. The calves stay with their mothers for many years. Each female may have two or three calves at different ages. When the males are fully grown at ten years, they may leave the herd to live on their own.

Cat behaviour

You can learn a lot about cats by watching how they behave. A cat may greet you by rubbing itself against your leg. The cat is rubbing its scent over you. This is its way of claiming ownership.

▲ *Beware! Puffed-out fur, an arched back and a straight tail mean that a cat is ready to attack.*

Friend or foe?

A cat uses its tail to communicate. A happy and friendly cat has a raised tail with the tip tilted to one side. A tail that is straight or arched, with the fur puffed out, means that a cat is scared. It is ready to attack or defend itself. A cat that swishes its tail from side to side is very irritated and about to attack. Ears are important, too. A happy cat points its ears forwards and up. A frightened cat presses its ears down flat.

◀ *A raised tail with the tip bent over is a sure sign that this cat is friendly.*

18

Meows and purrs

Cats can make more than 100 sounds, including meows, purrs, peeps, groans and growls. They purr when they are happy. A growl or a hiss is a warning that a cat is annoyed. Many owners come to know the meaning of these sounds. Cats can be very noisy when they call to each other at night. Their shrill cries are known as caterwauls.

Rough tongues

Cats like to keep themselves clean. They spend several hours each day licking their fur. A cat has a very rough tongue which it uses to smooth its fur and remove dirt. Because the cat has such a flexible body, it can reach every part with its tongue, except the head and face.

◀ *Cats are clean animals. They spend hours licking their fur.*

Ticks and fleas

Grooming is very important for some mammals. Monkeys, chimps and baboons pick out **ticks** and fleas from each other's fur. This keeps them clean, but it also helps the animals to feel close to each other.

▶ *A young baboon uses its fingers to pick out fleas from a baby baboon's fur.*

Living alone

Wild cats usually have a **territory**, or area of land, in which they live. They claim the territory as their own and defend it against other cats. The territory has to be large enough to supply the cat with food, water and shelter.

▲ *A male cat defends its territory by arching its back to make itself look larger.*

◄ *A cat marks its territory by rubbing its scent over walls and fences.*

Domestic cats, especially male cats, make their garden their territory. A cat walks around its garden, marking the boundary, or edge, with its **urine**. It rubs itself against fence posts and walls to leave its scent all over them. This is a warning to other cats that the garden is occupied. Male cats defend their territory by fighting other male cats that venture into the garden. Many cats suffer scratches and ripped ears in these cat fights.

Marking out territory

Many wild mammals mark out the boundary of their territory by leaving their scent on tree trunks and stones. A male tiger stands against a tree to rub his chest on the trunk. This way his scent is at the right height for other tigers to smell. Weasels, skunks and badgers produce a thick, oily and very smelly liquid called **musk**. They leave a little of this on stones and posts which other animals smell as they pass by.

▶ *Weasels leave their smelly musk on stones and logs.*

▶ *A tiger rubs its scent on a tree branch at the boundary of its territory.*

Finding a mate

A cat is fully grown by the time it is about six months old. A female cat is ready to **mate** at the age of about one year. Most cats mate and give birth to kittens during the spring and summer months.

▲ *A female cat is ready to have a litter when she is one year old.*

A cat's **pregnancy** lasts about nine weeks. For the first month, the cat does not look any different. Then her **abdomen** starts to swell. As the weeks pass, the mother cat's body becomes even larger as her unborn kittens grow. By the seventh week, you can see the kittens moving around inside her body when she lies down. She needs to eat a lot more than normal to feed her developing kittens.

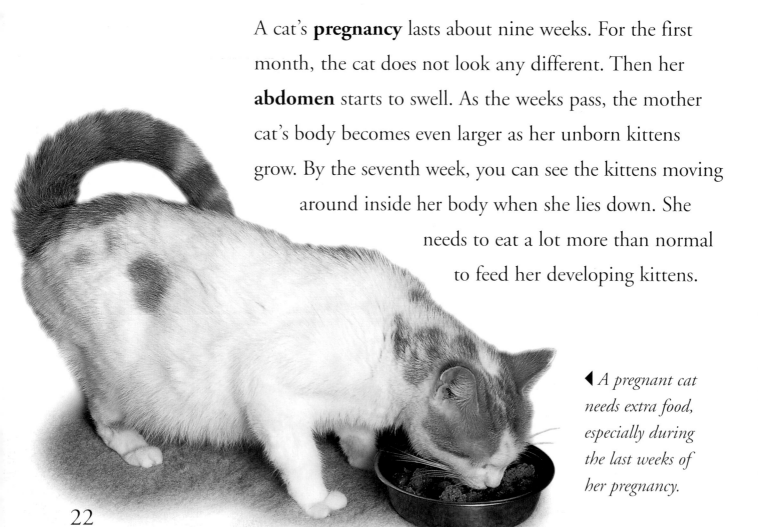

◀ *A pregnant cat needs extra food, especially during the last weeks of her pregnancy.*

22

◀ A lioness crouches down to show that she is ready to mate.

A female lion is ready to breed when she is about three years old, too. Her pregnancy lasts between 14 and 16 weeks. The newborn cubs are small and there are usually two or three in the litter.

Family life

Tigers living in the wild do not mate until they are three years old. The female's pregnancy lasts 14 weeks and she gives birth to a litter of two, three or four cubs. The cubs stay with her for about 18 months. When they leave their mother, they live close by for the next two years.

▶ Tiger cubs can be born at any time of the year.

▲ Two lionesses and a cub. Lion cubs cannot look after themselves fully until they are two years old.

Growing old

Cats can have a long life – up to 20 years. The record is held by a tabby cat called Ma which lived to the amazing age of 34 years.

▲ *Old cats sleep a lot and are much less active.*

Older cats are not as active as young cats. They spend much of the day asleep, and may put on weight as they take less exercise. As they grow older, cats may lose some of their teeth. They find it difficult to eat meat and may need softer food.

Their hair can become thin and they may develop skin problems. Some older cats suffer from **arthritis**. This is a disease that affects the **joints**, such as the hips and shoulders. The joints swell up and make walking, running and jumping painful.

Long-lived cats

Wild cats are long lived, too. Lions and tigers can reach 15 years of age in the wild, while cheetahs and leopards can live for 12 years. These cats may live to 20 years in **captivity**. An old lion stays in the pride if it remains healthy. But, if it is weakened by injury or disease, it is chased off by the younger males and left to die. Tigers live solitary lives. If an older tiger cannot catch enough food, it starves to death.

▼ *Elderly, weak lions are usually abandoned by the rest of the pride.*

▶ *Leopards usually live alone. They often rest in the branches of trees.*

Other mammals

There are more than 4500 different types of mammals – from tiny shrews and voles to huge elephants and whales. Most mammals live on land, but bats have wings and can fly. Whales, seals and dolphins live in water.

▲ *This Hanuman langur is a type of monkey found in India.*

▲ *The echidna lives in places where there are plenty of ants and termites to eat.*

The duck-billed platypus and the echidna belong to a group of mammals called monotremes. These are the most **primitive** mammals, and the only ones that lay eggs.

Kangaroos, koalas and wallabies are all marsupials. Marsupials give birth to tiny babies which crawl into their mother's pouch, where they continue to grow.

◀ *When a koala is seven months old, it leaves its mother's pouch and travels around on her back.*

Primates

Monkeys, lemurs, apes and humans are primates. Primates are very intelligent, because they have large brains for their body size. Many primates live in forests where their long limbs help them to move through the trees.

Marine mammals

Whales, dolphins and seals have flippers instead of legs and arms. Their bodies are torpedo shaped to help them swim through the water. They have a thick layer of fat, known as **blubber**, below their skin. This helps to keep them warm in cold water.

Ungulates

Horses, rhinoceroses, pigs, sheep, deer and elephants are all ungulates. These mammals look very different, but they all have hoofs and eat plants. Plant-eaters are called **herbivores**. They have teeth which are designed to chew plants and stomachs which can **digest** tough plant matter.

◀ *The body of a seal is the perfect shape for diving underwater.*

▼ *An ungulate, such as this rhino, is a mammal that has hoofs.*

Amazing mammals

- The largest mammal is the blue whale. It weighs more than 120 tonnes and its body is more than 26m long. Its heart is the size of a small car!

- The largest land mammal is the African elephant. Most adult elephants weigh between four and seven tonnes. The heaviest elephant on record weighed 12.2 tonnes. The smallest mammal is the Kitti's hog-nosed bat, or bumblebee bat, which weighs less than 2g.

- The longest-lived mammals are humans. A few humans have lived to more than 120 years of age. The elephant is next in line. One zoo elephant was 78 years old when it died.

- The fastest land mammal is the cheetah. It can reach speeds of up to 100 km/h over short distances. The fastest mammal over long distances is the pronghorn antelope of North America, which can run at speeds of up to 56 km/h over a distance of 6 km.

- The tallest mammal is the giraffe. It grows up to 6m tall, which allows the giraffe to reach the leaves at the tops of trees that other animals can't reach.

The life cycle of a cat

1 *A newborn kitten is deaf and its eyes are shut.*

2 *For the first week the kitten finds its way to its mother by smell and touch.*

8 *After a year a female cat is ready to mate and have kittens.*

3 *After ten days the kitten's eyes open.*

7 *After six months the cat is fully grown.*

4 *By six weeks the kitten has grown small teeth.*

6 *After eight weeks the kitten can look after itself. It leaves its mother to go to a new home.*

5 *The kitten is weaned on to solid foods.*

Glossary

abdomen In a mammal, the part of the body that contains the stomach, intestines, liver and kidneys.

arthritis A disease where the body's joints become swollen and painful.

blubber A thick layer of fat under the skin of marine mammals such as whales, seals and dolphins.

calf The name given to the young of some mammals, such as cattle, elephants, giraffes and whales.

canine A large, sharp tooth next to the incisors, used for tearing food.

captivity An animal in captivity is one that is kept in a zoo or as a pet.

carnivore An animal that eats other animals.

digest To change food into simpler forms that can be used by the body.

domestic Tame.

grazing animals Animals that eat grass, such as sheep, cows and horses.

grooming Cleaning and tidying fur.

herbivore An animal that eats only plants.

incisor A sharp, pointed tooth at the front of a mammal's mouth, used for biting, gnawing and nibbling.

instinct A natural feeling that an animal is born with and which helps it to survive.

joint The place where two bones are joined together.

litter All the babies born at one time to a cat, dog or other mammal.

mammal A type of animal that feeds its young on milk.

mate To pair or breed.

molar A large, flat tooth at the back of a mammal's mouth, used for grinding and chewing food.

musk A thick, oily, strong-smelling liquid produced by some animals to mark their territory.

nipple A small swelling on the front or underside of a mammal's body that produces milk.

predator An animal that hunts and kills other animals for food.

pregnancy The period in which unborn baby mammals develop inside the mother's body.

premolar A large tooth for chewing, between the canines and the molars.

prey Animals that are killed by other animals for food.

pride A group of lions.

primitive Simple, not very advanced.

retracted Pulled in.

savannah Wide, open grasslands in southern Africa.

sensitive Easily affected by something.

solitary Living alone.

suckle To suck milk from a nipple.

tabby A type of cat with wavy or striped fur, usually grey or brown.

territory The area of land where an animal lives.

tick A tiny animal with eight legs that attaches itself to the skin of a larger animal to suck its blood.

urine The yellow waste liquid that an animal or human passes from its body from time to time.

weaning Moving from a diet of milk to a diet of solid food.

Index